IMMIGRANTS AND
THE RIGHT TO STAY

IMMIGRANTS AND THE RIGHT TO STAY

Joseph H. Carens

A Boston Review Book

THE MIT PRESS Cambridge, Mass. London, England

MIT Press books may be purchased at special quantity
discounts for business or sales promotional use. For
information, please e-mail special_sales@mitpress.mit.edu or
write to Special Sales Department, The MIT Press,
55 Hayward Street, Cambridge, MA 02142.

This book was set in Adobe Garamond by *Boston Review*
and was printed and bound in the United States of America.

Library of Congress Cataloging-in-Publication Data
Carens, Joseph H.
Immigrants and the right to stay / Joseph H. Carens.
 p. cm.
"A Boston Review book."
Includes bibliographical references.
ISBN 978-0-262-01483-0 (hardcover : alk. paper)
1. Amnesty—Government policy—United States. 2. Illegal
aliens—United States. 3. United States—Emigration and
immigration—Government policy. I. Title.
JV6483.C37 2010
325.73—dc22

                                            2010020375

10 9 8 7 6 5 4 3 2 1

For Jenny, Michael, and Daniel

CONTENTS

I

The Case for Amnesty

MIGUEL SANCHEZ COULD NOT EARN enough to pay the bills in his hometown. He tried for several years to obtain a visa to come to the United States and was rejected every time. In 2000 he entered on foot with the help of a smuggler. He made his way to Chicago, where he had relatives and friends, and started working in construction, sending money to his father. Sanchez worked weekends at Dunkin Donuts and went to school in the evening to learn English. In 2002 he met an American-born U.S. citizen who lived in his neighborhood. They married in 2003, and now have a four-year-old son.

Sanchez, his wife, and son live under constant fear of his deportation. Driving to the funeral of a relative in another city causes high stress: a traffic stop or an accident can lead to Sanchez's removal from the country. Nor can the family travel by plane. Their son has never met his grandparents in Mexico. Meanwhile, they have an ordinary life in the neighborhood: they own a home and pay taxes; their child attends preschool, and they have become friends with other parents. Current U.S. law provides Sanchez and his family no feasible path to regularize his status.

Miguel Sanchez's story is true, but for a few identifying details. There are millions of similar stories in North America and Europe. Some 11 million irregular migrants—non-citizens living within a territory without official authorization—now reside in the United States.

The European numbers are smaller, but the reality is similar. People make their way across the southern Mediterranean or through Eastern Europe, or they arrive through authorized channels and overstay visas. Like Miguel Sanchez, they find work, have families, and live ordinary lives—ordinary, but for one dramatic difference: their vulnerability to deportation.

How should a liberal democracy respond to the vulnerability of irregular migrants? Should it expel irregular migrants whenever it finds them? Should it accept them as members of the community, at least after they have been present for an extended period, and grant them legal authorization to stay? Should it pursue some other alternative, with a path to permanent residence mixed with penalties and restrictions?

The right answer, I think, is a (qualified) version of the second alternative. Irregular migrants should be granted amnesty—allowed to remain with legal status as residents—if they have been settled for a long time. Some circumstances—arriving as children or marrying citizens or permanent residents—may accelerate or strengthen their moral claims to stay, but the most important consideration is the passage of time.

ALTHOUGH MOST READERS OF THIS BOOK are Americans (as I am myself, in addition to being Canadian), I pose a general question about liberal democracies, because they share some important principles and values. While particular features of American (or British or French or Canadian) legal tradition, history, and circumstances may affect our stance toward irregular migration, there are common moral commitments that limit the range of acceptable policies. It can be helpful to remind ourselves sometimes of the wider moral communities we belong to, and, as we will see, Americans have something to learn from Europeans in this area.

Most people think that the state has the right to determine whom it will admit and the right to apprehend and deport migrants who settle without official authorization. Let's accept that conventional view about states and borders as a premise and explore the question of whether a state nonetheless may sometimes be morally obliged to grant legal-resident status to irregular migrants. We will find that the claims of irregular migrants are strong, even on this conventional assumption.

MIGUEL SANCHEZ HAS BEEN IN THE UNITED States for almost ten years. Does that length of time affect his moral claim to remain? Some might argue that the passage of time is irrelevant. Some might even say that the longer the stay, the greater the blame and the more the irregular migrant deserves to be deported. In my view, the opposite is true: the longer the stay, the stronger the moral claim to remain.

Consider the case of Margaret Grimmond. Grimmond was born in the United States but moved to Scotland with her mother as a young child. At the age of 80, she left for a family vacation to Australia. It was her first time away from the United Kingdom, and she used a newly acquired American passport. When she returned, immigration officials told Grimmond that she was not legally entitled to stay and had four weeks to leave the country. In effect, she was identified as someone who had been an irregular migrant all those years, since she had never established a legal right to reside in the United Kingdom. And she clearly knew that she was not a British citizen since she had acquired an American passport for her trip.

Once the newspapers learned of the story— and it received international attention—Grimmond was allowed to remain. Whatever the legal technicalities of the case, the moral absurdity of forcing Grimmond to leave a place where she had lived so long was evident to all (apart from a few bureaucrats). She may have been an irregular migrant for all those years, but that clearly no longer mattered.

Grimmond had a moral right to stay for two reasons: she had arrived at a young age and she had stayed very long. Because Grimmond had arrived as a child, she was not responsible for the decision to settle in the United Kingdom. Being raised there made her a member of U.K. society, regardless of her legal status. The importance of such social membership was implicitly recognized even in the British Nationality Act of 1981, which restricted access to citizenship in a number of ways. Among other things, the law abolished the traditional rule (still followed in the United States and Canada) that anyone born on the territory was a citizen (the *jus soli* rule). Automatic acquisition of citizenship was limited to the children of citizens and permanent residents. Nevertheless, the Act made an exception for anyone who was born in Britain and raised there during the first ten years of her life. It appears that the United Kingdom did not want to deport people with such strong ties to the country.

The rationale behind the British Nationality Act's ten-year rule is compelling, but neither it nor the laws of most other states recognize that the same rationale applies even more forcefully to children who are not born in a country but who spend ten years of their childhood there. After all, the ten years from six to sixteen (or from eight to eighteen) are even more important in creating a substantial connection to the country where one lives than the first ten years of life. The later years of childhood are the most important ones from society's perspective—the formative years of education and wider socialization. Human beings who have been raised in a democratic society become members of that society: not recognizing their social membership is cruel and unjust. It is morally wrong to force someone to leave the place where she was raised, where she received her social formation, and where she has her most important human connections, just because her parents brought her there without official authorization. Yet current legal rules in North America and Europe threaten many young people in just this way.

The principle that irregular status becomes irrelevant over time is clearest for those who arrive as young children. But the second element in Grimmond's case—the sheer length of time she had lived in the United Kingdom—is also powerful. What if Grimmond had arrived at twenty rather than two? Would anyone really think that this difference would make it acceptable to deport her 60 years later? Grimmond's case clearly illustrates that there is some period of time beyond which it is unreasonable to deport people who arrived illegally.

How long is too long? What if Grimmond had been 60 rather than 80? Would that have diminished her claim to stay? I assume not. What if she had been 40? The poignancy of the case certainly diminishes, but the underlying principle remains: there is something deeply wrong in forcing people to leave a place where they have lived for a long time. Most people form their deepest human connections where they live—it becomes home. Even if someone has arrived only as an adult, it seems cruel and inhumane to uproot a person who has spent fifteen or twenty years as a contributing member of society in the name of enforcing immigration restrictions. The harm is entirely out of proportion to the wrong of illegal entry.

When her ordeal was over, Grimmond expressed relief: she had "worried," she said, "about moving to America because I don't have any friends or family there." Normally we do not think of moving to the United States as a terrible prospect. But think about the fear and anxiety Grimmond must have felt, and then about the reality of irregular migrants, who can be and are deported even after very long periods of residence. Grimmond was lucky because her case attracted so much public attention. Had it not, the immigration bureaucracy might well have sent her "home."

Grimmond's case poses a particularly difficult challenge for those who would uphold at all costs the state's right to deport irregular migrants, but her claims are not unique. Hiu Lui Ng arrived in New York at the age of seventeen with his parents. After his tourist visa expired, he applied for asylum and obtained a work permit while his application was reviewed. Although his application for asylum was eventually denied, he managed over the years to attend a local high school and then a community college, developing technical skills as a computer engineer. He married an American citizen, had two children, and acquired a house in Queens and a job at the Empire State Building. In 2007 he came to the attention of immigration officials when, following bad legal advice, he applied for a green card. Immigration and Customs Enforcement detained him and set out to deport him. In the end, Ng died before he could be deported. His story appeared in *The New York Times* primarily because of the ways in which he had been mistreated and neglected by those supervising his detention—he suffered from a broken spine and liver cancer that was diagnosed only five days before it killed him. But why was the United States trying to deport Hiu Lui Ng in the first place? He was an American in every respect that mattered, except legal status.

Ng's claim not to be deported, like Grimmond's, has two elements, though the details are different. Ng did not arrive here as a young child (although he was brought by his parents), so his early social formation did not take place in the United States. On the other hand, Ng, like Miguel Sanchez, was married to an American citizen. Marriage creates deep ties, not only with the person one marries but also with the communities to which that person belongs.

Living with one's family is a fundamental human interest. The right to family life is recognized as a basic human right in various European laws, and concern for family values has played a central role in American political rhetoric in recent decades. All liberal democratic states recognize the principle of family reunification, i.e., that citizens and legal residents should generally be able to have their foreign spouses and minor children join them and that this takes priority over the normal discretionary power that the state exercises over immigration. (In fact, Ng was applying for residency on this basis.) Once Ng was married to an American citizen, his ties to the United States, his interest in living here, and his spouse's interest in living here all assumed a new importance and greatly outweighed any interest the state had in deporting him in order to enforce its immigration laws. Even if the state is generally entitled to enforce its immigration laws (as I assume here), it is not right to do so without regard for the harm done in such a case. If an irregular migrant marries a citizen or a legal permanent resident, he or she should no longer be subject to deportation.

In addition to the claim that he had to remain in the United States because of his marriage to an American citizen, Ng had a powerful claim to stay simply because he had already been in the United States so long and thus had become a member of society. Unlike Grimmond, he had not been present for over seven decades, but he had lived peacefully in the United States for fifteen years, getting an education, working, building social connections, creating a life.

Fifteen years is a long time in a human life. In fifteen years, connections grow: to spouses and partners, sons and daughters, friends and neighbors and coworkers, people we love and people we hate. Experiences accumulate: birthdays and braces, tones of voice and senses of humor, public parks and corner stores, the shape of the streets and the way the sun shines through the leaves, the smell of flowers and the sounds of local accents, the look of the stars and the taste of the air—all that gives life its purpose and texture. We sink deep roots over fifteen years, and these roots matter even if we were not authorized to plant ourselves in the first place. The moral importance of Ng's social membership ought to have outweighed the importance of enforcing immigration restrictions.

THE MORAL RIGHT OF STATES TO APPRE-
hend and deport irregular migrants erodes with
the passage of time. As irregular migrants become more and more settled, their membership
in society grows in moral importance, and the
fact that they settled without authorization becomes correspondingly less relevant. At some
point a threshold is crossed, and they acquire a
moral claim to have their actual social membership legally recognized. They should acquire a
legal right of permanent residence and all the
rights that go with that, including eventual access to citizenship.

How can migrants become members of
society without legal authorization? They can
because social membership does not depend
upon official permission: this is the crux of
my argument. People who live and work and
raise their families in a society become members, whatever their legal status. That is why
we find it hard to expel them when they are

discovered. Their presence may be against the law, but they are not criminals like thieves and murderers. It would be wrong to deport them once they have become members, even if we have good reasons for wanting to make them leave and trying to prevent others like them from coming.

Over time, the circumstances of entry grow less important. Eventually, they become altogether irrelevant. That was recognized in Europe in the 1970s, when people who had originally been admitted as "guest workers," with the explicit expectation that they would leave after a limited period, nevertheless were granted resident status. Of course, the guest workers' claim to stay was somewhat stronger than that of irregular migrants, because the guest workers were invited. But this difference is not decisive: after all, the guest workers' permanent settlement contradicted the terms of their initial admission. What was morally important was that they had established themselves firmly as members of society.

MY ARGUMENT THAT TIME MATTERS CUTS in both directions. If there is a threshold of time after which it is wrong to expel settled irregular migrants, then there is also some period of time before this threshold is crossed. How much time must pass before irregular migrants acquire a strong moral claim to stay? Or from the opposite perspective, how long does the state have to apprehend and expel irregular migrants?

There is no clear answer to that question. The growth of the moral claim is continuous, although at some point it becomes strong enough that further time is irrelevant. The examples I have cited suggest that fifteen or twenty years are much more than enough. Ten years seems to me like a maximum, and I would think that five years of settled residence without any criminal convictions should normally be sufficient to establish anyone as a responsible member of society. On the other hand, it seems plausible to claim that a year or two is not long enough.

The policy implication of this analysis is that states should move away from the practice of granting occasional large-scale amnesties or providing a right to stay on a case-by-case basis through appeal to humanitarian considerations. Instead, states should establish an individual right for migrants to transform their status from irregular to legal after a fixed period of residence, such as five to seven years.

Proving length of residence can be a problem, but past practice shows that this difficulty is not insuperable. For example, France had for many years a policy that granted an entitlement to legal-resident status to anyone who could show that he or she had lived there for at least ten years. When a right-wing government came to power in 2003, the policy was made much more discretionary and restrictive, but the change was spurred by ideological hostility to immigration, not by evidence that the previous policy increased the level of irregular migration or created other problems.

Similarly, for a long time, the United States routinely limited deportations of people who had lived here for some time, as Mae Ngai reminds us in her contribution to this volume. For much of the twentieth century, American officials were able to grant permanent-resident status to migrants (including irregular migrants) who could establish that they had lived in the country continuously for ten years and met certain other requirements regarding employment, the lack of a criminal record, and so on. The same rule gave positive weight to family ties to American citizens and residents. Unlike the French policy, the American one always depended on the discretion of officials.

It did not give migrants a legal entitlement to the regularization of their status, and the discretion was often exercised in a racially biased manner, as Ngai points out.

Nevertheless, this form of amnesty was granted fairly often. Like the French policy, it recognized the moral logic I defend here: that people become members of our community over time, even if they settle without authorization, and that this membership should be recognized by law. In recent years opponents of immigration have placed legislative restrictions on the exercise of this discretionary authority, and political dynamics have further limited its use. It is much more difficult for irregular migrants to gain legal status under this provision than it once was. Still, the principle remains on the books: the passage of time creates a moral claim to stay.

Identifying a specific moment after which irregular migrants have a legal right to remain inevitably involves an element of arbitrariness.

No one can pretend that choosing five years rather than four or six involves any question of fundamental principle. It is more a matter of the social psychology of coordination, given the need to settle on one point within a range. But if one asks why five years rather than one or fifteen, it is easier to make the case that one is too short and fifteen too long, given common understandings of the ways in which people settle into the societies where they live.

Some people are puzzled by the weight in my approach given to the passage of time, rather than the actual range and intensity of the migrant's social ties in the new society. Is it really right to pay attention only to the passage of time, "the sheer number of years" as Jean Elshtain puts it in her contribution?

There is merit in this concern. Individuals form attachments and become members of a community at different rates. And the harm done to someone in forcing him or her to leave will vary too. It is not the passage of time *per se* that matters but what that normally signifies about the development of a human life. It is appropriate, for example, to give special weight to certain factors: social formation in the country in which one seeks regularized status, marriage to a citizen or legal resident, a clean record and a history of employment. But it would be a mistake to try to establish a much wider range of criteria of belonging and an especially big mistake to grant more discretion to officials in judging whether individual migrants have passed the threshold of belonging that should entitle them to stay.

My opposition to a more complicated and more discretionary approach is partly a matter of efficiency. When it comes to assigning legal rights and responsibilities, like the right to vote or marry, a state does not normally inquire into the capacities of each person. Rather it establishes rules that tie the possession of rights and responsibilities to an objective measure of the passage of time. The gain from a more detailed inquiry into individual capacities is much too small to warrant the expenditure of public resources that it would require. The same would be true of any effort to make individual determinations about depth of membership for irregular migrants.

More importantly, however, to let officials probe the degree to which a particular person belongs would run afoul of the normative commitment of liberal democratic states to respect individuals. We have every reason to worry that discretionary criteria would be interpreted and applied (whether consciously or not) in a discriminatory manner. In addition, there is something presumptuous in imagining that an official can make nuanced judgments about how deeply a person belongs to the society in which she lives.

THE ARGUMENT THAT I HAVE BEEN DE-
veloping is a constraint on the state's right to
control immigration, not a repudiation of it.
Nothing in my argument denies a government's
moral and legal right to prevent entry in the
first place and to deport those who settle without authorization, so long as these expulsions
take place at a relatively early stage of residence.
At the same time, the case I have advanced is
only a minimalist one (though doubtless it will
not appear so to many). I have identified only
some of the general moral constraints upon
the deportation and exclusion of irregular migrants, not all of the moral considerations that
might generate responsibilities to irregular migrants or limit the state's right to deport.

One such consideration is the claim that
states are complicit in irregular migration.
Many argue that rich, liberal democratic states
do not actually want to exclude irregular migrants, despite loud public pronouncements

to that effect. From the state's perspective, it is precisely their irregular status that makes them desirable as workers: their vulnerability means they are tractable and easy to exploit. If this is true, then it undermines the argument that irregular migrants are present without the consent of the political community and so not entitled to the same rights as legally authorized migrants. If a state covertly encourages migrants to enter, it owes them the same status and legal rights to which they would be entitled if they were recruited openly. Even if it is not a matter of the state explicitly recruiting irregular migrants, but only of failing to enforce immigration laws and controls when it could do so, the state bears considerable responsibility for the results of its inaction.

State complicity in irregular migration reinforces the moral case for amnesty. And this is not just a point of principle. In Spain, Italy, and even the United States, recognition of the state's complicity in irregular migration movements has in the past helped generate public support for regularization policies for irregular migrants.

But we should be careful not to overuse the complicity argument for three reasons. First, the argument that the state is complicit in irregular migration only makes sense when there is scope for state action (or inaction) to make some difference in the number of irregular migrants. To the extent that irregular migration flows are determined by structural factors beyond the state's control, as some analysts argue, the state cannot be held responsible for failing to prevent the entry and settlement of the irregular migrants. We can criticize state policies for being ineffective or counterproductive, but not for complicity.

Second, we cannot simply infer the state's complicity from the fact that some employers within the receiving society want to hire irregular migrants. No state can be held responsible for the desires or actions of every citizen or corporation within its jurisdiction. To establish complicity, it is necessary to show that the state is facilitating or permitting irregular migration, despite its formal policies—for example, by relaxing enforcement efforts against migrant workers during the hiring season. This is sometimes the case, but not always.

Third, one cannot charge a state with complicity simply because of its failure to deter unauthorized immigration. Every enforcement effort has some failure rate. In some cases a state's effort to prevent unauthorized immigration and to expel those who are discovered may legitimately be hampered by other considerations. For example, some argue that efforts in the United States and Southern Europe to keep people out already go too far because they cost too many lives. If border officials were to cut back on some of these measures to save lives, we should not turn around and accuse them of complicity in letting the migrants in. Similarly, the mere presence of visa overstayers does not by itself show that states are encouraging unauthorized migration. Visitors from poor states to rich ones already face restrictions on entry that are severe and discriminatory. Tightening those restrictions further because a few of the visitors do not leave when they are supposed to would impose too high a cost to be a defensible way of restricting irregular migration.

Various moral considerations will always limit the ways in which states may try to control irregular migration, even if one accepts the legitimacy of the goal itself. But these limits and the surplus of irregular migrants generated by them do not represent evidence of a state's complicity in irregular migration or undercut its right to try to restrict unauthorized settlement. Actual complicity, in the form of deliberately lax or fluctuating enforcement, does undercut the state's right to deport irregular migrants.

Another moral consideration that limits the ways in which the state may pursue the goal of preventing irregular migration is the state's duty to provide irregular migrants with a variety of legal rights and protections, despite their irregular status. States should, for example, protect every person within their jurisdiction against violence and theft. This is a basic human right, and the state is obliged to protect it for all those within its jurisdiction, regardless of whether they are citizens or residents or visitors, regardless of their immigration statuses and regardless of how long they have been present.

Basic human rights derive simply from one's status as a human being and the state's responsibility to protect them comes simply from one's presence within its jurisdiction. In that sense, these moral claims are quite different from the moral claim to amnesty, which emerges from a person's social membership over time. For that reason, it is not self-contradictory (as Linda Bosniak claims in this volume) to say that irregular migrants are entitled to basic human rights even though they are subject to deportation.

Bosniak rightly observes that vulnerability to deportation makes irregular migrants reluctant to assert their human rights or to seek legal remedies when these rights are violated, because they fear exposing their status to the authorities. I agree with Bosniak that my amnesty proposal does not fully solve this problem, since these violations may occur before migrants would be eligible for amnesty.

There is a way to address this issue without simply granting amnesty to migrants, regardless of how long they have been present. We can build a legal firewall between immigration enforcement and the protection of migrants' legal rights, such that no information gathered by those responsible for protecting and realizing migrants' fundamental rights can be used for immigration enforcement purposes. We ought to guarantee that people will be able to exercise their basic human rights without exposing themselves to apprehension and deportation. If irregular migrants are victims of a crime or witnesses to one, they should be able to go to the police, report the crime, and serve as witnesses without fear that this will increase the chances of their being arrested and deported. If they need emergency health care, they should be able to seek help without worrying that the hospital will disclose their identity to those responsible for enforcing immigration laws. A firewall approach will help to make migrants' rights real, rather than purely formal.*

---

* I have discussed the firewall approach in more detail in "The Rights of Irregular Migrants." *Ethics & International Affairs* 22, no. 2 (2008): 163–186. There I spell out more fully what rights should receive this sort of firewall protection and why.

There are tensions between pursuing deportation and protecting the rights of irregular migrants, but there are always tensions between enforcing rules and protecting the rights of people suspected of violating those rules. We know from experience that we can manage these tensions reasonably well. For example, the United States has a rule prohibiting the use of illegally obtained evidence in criminal trials. This makes the right to basic legal protections against unlawful search much more effective than it would be otherwise. A firewall approach, like the exclusionary rule regarding tainted evidence, would make a big difference to the lives of those protected by it, dramatically reducing their vulnerability and exploitation, even if it did not work perfectly.

WHY NOT GO FURTHER? WHY NOT GRANT amnesty to everyone who wants it regardless of length of stay? Bosniak believes that my acceptance of the premise that states have a right to control admissions reflects a retreat from an earlier, more idealistic argument on behalf of open borders to a more "realistic" and "pragmatic" position here.

In some respects I am pleased to hear my argument for amnesty characterized as realistic and pragmatic. That is certainly not the way everyone sees it. Nevertheless, I cannot accept Bosniak's analysis.

My approach to the question of amnesty is not primarily a concession to political realities. It is rather an attempt to engage in a respectful conversation with people who believe deeply in the state's right to control admissions. I still believe in my open borders argument, but in democratic life, we have an obligation to seek common ground, to look for areas of agreement in the midst of our disagreements. One of the ways of doing that is to accept others' views as premises in order to limit the range of issues under debate in a given moment. That is what I have done here. Those who think that justice ultimately requires open borders and those who think that states are morally entitled to control entry should both be able to agree that, once people have settled for a long time, they become members and should be recognized as such. This is not a covert argument for open borders because it is an argument about membership, not universal rights. The arguments that I have advanced about the ways in which living in a society creates moral claims over time are entirely independent of the argument for open borders.

IF BOSNIAK WORRIES THAT THE CASE I have made for amnesty is too pragmatic, others worry that it is not pragmatic enough. It is true, as I said before, that my argument here is not primarily driven by pragmatic concerns. As Douglas Massey rightly contends in his contribution to this volume, any serious attempt to address the broad problem of unauthorized migration at the level of public policy must take into account the history and specific features of the problem in a particular context. I am persuaded by Massey and others that the relationship with Mexico is the key issue for the United States in this area. I am generally sympathetic to Massey's analysis and his ideas for solutions, but I do not pretend to be an expert on the policy issues. My goal is not to offer comprehensive policy proposals but to highlight the moral dimensions of one aspect of the issue: the case for amnesty.

Some think that my focus on moral arguments is unwise, however. Alex Aleinikoff points out that there are moral arguments against amnesty as well as for it. He suggests that we should limit ourselves to pragmatic arguments for regularization, such as the costs and social disruption entailed in trying to deport eleven million irregular migrants from the United States. I disagree. I endorse Aleinikoff's pragmatic case for amnesty, but I think that there is a strong principled case to be made as well. For too long advocates of legalization have relied almost entirely on the pragmatic case, leaving moral arguments to those who oppose legalization in the name of fairness and respect for the law. I am deliberately taking the opposite approach, challenging the assumption that irregular migrants do not deserve legal status and that the only case for granting it is an appeal to practicality and perhaps compassion. It is important to articulate the reasons why irregular migrants deserve legal status as a matter of justice. That is why I have embraced the term "amnesty," a term that opponents of legalization use with derision and supporters normally avoid.

So far, I have concentrated primarily on the positive case for amnesty. But the moral arguments against the idea of granting legal status to long-settled irregular migrants deserve a hearing.

Aleinikoff himself mentions one such argument: "the moral claim of a self-governing people to determine who should be members of their polity." Aleinikoff is right that there is a moral claim to collective self-governance, but this claim is not unconstrained. The question of who belongs should not be seen as simply a matter of discretionary choice, whether made by political authorities or even by the majority of the citizenry. It is a sad truth of our history that popular majorities, political authorities, and even our courts of law have said at various times that Americans of African or Asian or indigenous descent could not be full legal members of our society because the self-governing people refused to consent to their belonging. Ngai's contribution reminds us of the specific ways in which that pattern has played itself out with respect to deportation and amnesty in American history. We all recognize the injustice of those racial and ethnic exclusions today. My claim is that our collective refusal to recognize long-settled irregular migrants as Americans is also unwarranted, their exclusion also an injustice. This injustice is not rendered acceptable by the fact that it now applies to all irregular migrants and not just to racial minorities. It is not morally acceptable even if it has the support of a democratic majority.

Another moral objection to amnesty is that allowing irregular migrants to stay is unfair to foreigners who have played by the rules and waited in line for admission. Stated abstractly, this argument seems to have force, but when one considers the reality, it is much less persuasive. In many democratic states, there is no real admissions line for those without close family ties or special credentials. Even in countries such as the United States and Canada that encourage legal immigration, there are almost no immigration lines for unskilled workers without close family ties to current citizens or residents. Most of those who settle as irregular migrants would have no possibility of getting in through any authorized channel. To say that they should stand in a line which does not exist or does not move is disingenuous.

Perhaps the strongest moral objection to amnesty is that it rewards lawbreaking. It is true that the rules governing immigration are laws, but so are the rules governing automobile traffic. We don't describe drivers who exceed the speed limit as illegal drivers or criminals. In most states, violations of immigration law are treated as an administrative matter, not a criminal offense. If immigration violations are not criminal offences, those who violate immigration laws cannot reasonably be described as criminals.

In any event we all recognize that laws vary enormously in the harms they seek to prevent and the order they seek to maintain. Laws against murder are more important than laws against theft, laws against theft more important than laws regulating automobile traffic. The laws restricting immigration are a lot more like traffic regulations than like laws prohibiting murder and theft. These laws serve a useful social function, but that function can be served reasonably well even if there is a fair amount of deviance and most rule-breakers are never caught. For enforcement purposes, it makes sense to focus on the really dangerous violators—those driving drunk or so recklessly as to endanger lives in the case of traffic laws, those who engage in terrorism or crime in the case of immigration laws. For run-of-the-mill violations (ordinary speeding, irregular migration for work), just having the rules in place and occasional enforcement will maintain order at a sufficient level.

Settling without authorization violates immigration laws, but that does not mean that we should punish people many years after the fact. As Ngai has argued elsewhere, there is a parallel between statutes of limitations for criminal offenses and a policy of not deporting long-settled irregular migrants. Most states recognize that the passage of time matters morally, at least for less serious criminal violations. If a person has not been arrested and charged within a specified period (often three to five years), legal authorities may no longer pursue her for that offense.

Why do states establish statutes of limitations? Because it is not right to make people live indefinitely with a threat of serious legal consequences hanging over their heads for some long-past action, except for the most serious sorts of offenses. Keeping the threat in place for a long period does not enhance deterrence and causes great harm to the individual—more than is warranted by the original offense. If we are prepared to let time erode the state's power to pursue actual crimes, it makes even more sense to let time erode the power of the state to pursue immigration violations, which are not normally treated as crimes and should not be viewed as crimes.

In a related vein, we should be wary of efforts to criminalize actions that irregular migrants take simply to live ordinary lives. Most jurisdictions have criminal laws prohibiting identity theft and the use of false documentation. These are usually sensible laws intended to prevent fraud. Of course, irregular migrants often provide false information to satisfy administrative or legal requirements. For example, they may provide a social security number that is not their own to an employer who uses this to deduct taxes from their pay. In most such cases, the irregular migrants are only trying to conceal their presence and are not engaged in deception designed to harm others. They pay their taxes, even when they are not entitled to the benefits that taxpayers normally receive (such as Social Security or unemployment compensation). Their actions may be technical violations of laws against identity theft and the use of false documents, but they are not normally the kinds of actions those laws were intended to prevent. Treating irregular migrants as criminals under these laws, as some authorities in the United States have been doing, is an abuse of the legal process.

The state does have the power to make irregular migrants the targets of laws designed to protect against fraud, just as it has the power to make violations of immigration laws a criminal offense. But if we weigh the harm criminalization aims to prevent against the social costs that criminalization incurs, we see that it makes no sense.

A final moral challenge to the case for amnesty is the claim that we have to choose between granting legal status to irregular migrants and providing assistance to "fellow citizens who continue to suffer racial discrimination, wanton neglect, and outright rejection," as Carol Swain puts it in this book. Swain is not the only person to make this argument. I share their concern for disadvantaged citizens, but I think that trying to improve the lot of disadvantaged citizens by deporting long-settled irregular migrants is a fundamental mistake.

First, if one accepts the claim that irregular migrants are (at some point) members who are entitled to legal status, then it is simply wrong to deny them that status for the sake of some other disadvantaged group. Excluding members from a legal status to which they are morally entitled is not a morally permissible policy option. This sort of reprehensible rationale was used to justify the legal subordination of African Americans for generations. Their exclusion was necessary, it was said, to improve the lot of poor whites.

Trying to deport settled irregular migrants is not an effective way to improve the situation of the least skilled among current citizens and legal residents. The firewall I have proposed would do much more to reduce the conflict between irregular migrants and disadvantaged citizens: enabling irregular migrants to join unions and to receive the minimum wage and other job-related protections would make them less vulnerable to exploitation and would thus reduce employers' incentives to seek out irregular migrants in preference to citizens and legal residents.

Finally, it is a mistake to divide disadvantaged groups and to set them against one another instead of building alliances to promote common interests. In this regard, I find it ironic that Swain evokes Martin Luther King's "I have a dream" speech in her critique. King was an advocate for solidarity among the poor and the dispossessed. He urged us to confront injustice wherever we found it. If Swain actually believes that King would be on the side of Lou Dobbs, Glenn Beck, and the "mostly Republican members of Congress" who have opposed efforts to include long-settled irregular migrants as legal members of the American community, then her understanding of his life and work is very different from mine.

SOME READERS MAY FIND THEMSELVES PERsuaded by my moral arguments but worried that an amnesty for long-term residents would encourage others to come without authorization. We should not dismiss this concern, though neither should we accept at face value every claim about the incentive effects of an amnesty for long-settled migrants. The actual effect of a rolling amnesty such as I have proposed is an empirical question dependent on a variety of factors. It is worth recalling that the French had such a policy in effect for years, and it did not open the floodgates. The more important point, however, is that an amnesty policy by itself is not a solution to all of the problems raised by irregular migration. There are many strategies for addressing the wider issue. As I noted above, any satisfactory approach will be contextually specific and will have many components from trade policy to visa allocations. I am just trying to draw attention to the moral principles that should govern one aspect of the wider problem: the treatment of long-settled irregular migrants.

Even if we accept the state's right to control immigration as a basic premise, that right is not absolute and unqualified. Over time an irregular migration status becomes morally irrelevant while the harm it inflicts grows. The state's right to deport weakens as the migrants become members of society. Liberal democratic states should recognize that fact by institutionalizing an automatic transition to legal status for irregular migrants who have settled for an extended period.

II

Forum

Mae M. Ngai

JOSEPH CARENS OFFERS A PERSUASIVE case for granting amnesty to unauthorized migrants. He argues that liberal democracies should acknowledge the social ties that migrants establish over time, which make them de facto members of society, even if they lack formal legal status. The longer migrants stay in the United States, the stronger their moral claim to remain. In effect,

Carens says, the better answer to the misalignment of social inclusion and unlawful status is legalization, not deportation.

Carens writes from the standpoint of the ethical commitments that undergird liberal democratic societies. I would like to add a historical argument. The history of American immigration policy suggests two lessons of current relevance. First, as long as we have had restrictions on immigration, we have had provisions for both deportation *and* legalization. Carens's argument is worthy, but it also is not new; legalization has always been based on the same principles: length of stay and familial ties to citizens. Second, there is a rough correlation between race and legalization. From the late nineteenth century through the middle of the twentieth, the United States established myriad policies that enabled some irregular migrants from Europe to legalize their status, but harsh policies toward those from China and Mexico.

From the time of the founding of the republic through most of the nineteenth century, immigration to the United States was normatively open. It may be hard for us today to imagine a system with no passports, visas, quotas, green cards, border patrol, deportations. The first restrictive immigration laws were the Chinese exclusion laws, passed by Congress in 1875 and 1882, first barring "Mongolian" prostitutes and then all Chinese laborers. Enforcement included both extreme interrogation of new arrivals and deportation of those without legal status. In 1892 Congress required legally resident Chinese to carry a permit; failure to produce it on demand was punishable by a year's imprisonment at hard labor followed by deportation—unless one could produce three white witnesses to vouch for one's legal status. The U.S. Supreme Court upheld the permit requirement, ruling in *Fong Yue Ting v. United States* that aliens entered and remained only by "the license, permission, and sufferance of Congress." The court did strike down the provision for imprisonment at hard labor.

In 1882 Congress also passed the first general immigration law, which excluded from the United States convicts, lunatics, idiots, and persons likely to become public charges. By World War I the list of excludable categories grew to include contract laborers, persons with "loathsome and contagious disease," prostitutes, polygamists, and anarchists. These exclusions indexed concern over potential drains on the public coffers and fears of moral contaminants. The first deportation law, passed in 1891, authorized the removal of aliens who within one year of arrival became public charges from causes existing prior to landing. The expense of deportation was borne by the steamship company that originally brought the unwanted immigrant. Deportation was thus conceived as appropriate only for persons with limited length of stay in the country. Even as Congress extended the statutes of limitations on removal to five years for certain categories in the early twentieth century, it still hewed to this basic principle. However, that appreciation of immigrant settlement and incorporation did not extend to the Chinese, whose exclusion was based on a racial logic that Chinese were inherently unassimilable. There was no statute of limitation for deporting unauthorized Chinese.

When Congress passed the first *numerical* restrictions on European immigration in the 1920s, it provided no statutes of limitations for violations of the quota laws, evincing a different attitude toward trespass against the nation's sovereignty than it had toward individual qualification. By the early 1930s there was public outcry over the deportation of immigrants, especially those of European origin with longtime residence in the United

States. Frances Perkins, who as Secretary of Labor was responsible for enforcing the immigration laws, devised various administrative mechanisms that allowed for the legalization of irregular migrants. By the 1940s and '50s Congress passed legislation for suspension of deportation and legalization of status in cases of long-term residence, marriage to a citizen or a legal immigrant, and where deportation would result in "hardship" to the deportee or to family members left behind. The data suggest that far more Europeans were regularized under these programs than were Latinos or Asians. But both racial advantage and disadvantage were often leavened by ideology: the two big "red scares" of the twentieth century, after World War I and after World War II, especially targeted European-immigrant radicals. During the cold war, the Immigration and Naturalization Service (INS) deported unauthorized Chinese in the United States who were leftists, while offering legalization to unauthorized Chinese who foreswore association with communism.

The imposition of numerical limits on immigration from countries of the Western Hemisphere under the Hart-Celler Act of 1965 led to an upsurge of unauthorized migration from Mexico and Central America. There were two responses: on the one hand, nativist outcry against illegal aliens and, on the other hand, mobilization by a growing Latino political constituency for recognition and inclusion. The 1986 Immigration Reform and Control Act responded to these competing interests with a compromise—amnesty for the undocumented, greater border enforcement to prevent future unauthorized entry, and employer sanctions to prevent employment of irregular migrants (this latter provision was never seriously enforced). During these years the INS adopted a rationalized method for granting suspensions of deportation, involving a balance of equities that weighed the seriousness of one's offense against one's length of residence in the United States, familial and community ties, evidence of reform in the case of criminals, etc.

At the same time, the meaning of "hardship" steadily narrowed so that by the 1990s it was virtually useless as grounds for voiding a deportation order. Indeed the 1996 immigration laws (passed just as Congress was ending "welfare as we know it") made removal *mandatory* for nearly all cases of unauthorized presence, with no administrative discretion or judicial review. America's long history of practicing both deportation and legalization pretty much came to an end. The United States now only deports people. Amnesty, no stranger to the history of immigration policy, is now considered politically unthinkable. In fact, some of our older policies—statutes of limitations on unauthorized presence and mechanisms on the books for individuals to adjust their status—are actually more sensible than one-time amnesty programs because they serve as built-in correctives that prevent the accretion of a large unauthorized population.

When the Supreme Court stated in 1893 that Congress had the absolute authority to summarily expel Chinese migrants, that authority applied to *all* immigrants, at least in theory. In practice, however, immigration policy was much more forgiving toward unauthorized migrants from Europe. For a time, during the long civil rights era, Asians and Latinos were able to tap into that tradition. But that inclusionary impulse has since given way to exclusionary nativism, in which anxiety over migrant illegality has been arguably a proxy for racism against Latinos. But, in a twist of contemporary colorblindness, it also has become virtually impossible for all unauthorized migrants, regardless of national origin, to legalize their status. In a sense, Justice David

Brewer's dissent against arbitrary deportation in *Fong Yue Ting* has come to pass: "It is true," he wrote, that "this statute is directed only against the obnoxious Chinese, but, if the power exists, who shall say it will not be exercised tomorrow against other classes and other people?"

Carol M. Swain

JOSEPH CARENS ARGUES THAT STATES should exchange large-scale amnesties, case-by-case adjudications, and mass deportations for an immigration policy that rewards length of residence by granting special status to those illegal immigrants who have lived in the county the longest without detection. Long-term violators, he argues, have gained special membership rights and ought to be allowed to stay because it would be cruel and immoral to ask them to leave. Although Carens readily concedes that allowing long-term law-breakers to remain could be considered unfair to other immigrants, he contends that their years of residence make them members of our community worthy of amnesty.

As an intellectual exercise, Carens's analysis is compelling and worth pondering, especially when he introduces us to Miguel Sanchez and his quest for a better life that includes illegal entry via a smuggler, illegal employment in construction, eventual marriage to an American citizen, and the birth of a son on U.S. soil. Sanchez lives in constant fear of detection because he knows that any brush with the law might result in his deportation. Carens notes that U.S. law provides Sanchez and his family, "no feasible path to regularize his status."

While Sanchez's decision to enter the country illegally and remain seems perfectly rational,

Carens's use of his story as part of a defense of amnesty loses some of its moral force because of his failure to take into consideration the impact of illegal immigration on the most vulnerable members of American society: native-born Americans and legal immigrants with low skills and low levels of education.

Who are the people harmed? Obviously, it is not university professors, members of Congress, journalists, lawyers, or doctors. The most vulnerable people are U.S.-born blacks and Hispanics with high school educations or less. Unlike Carens, who ignores these groups, I would argue that their moral claim to justice trumps the moral case of Miguel Sanchez and the unknown millions who are in the country illegally and have taken jobs and opportunities to which they were not entitled.

Let me tell you about Joe Johnson, an African-American descendant of slaves, who graduated from high school and eventually landed a dream job at a factory in Virginia. After over-coming initial racism, he worked himself up to a supervisory role earning twelve dollars an hour. Joe married, had three children, and owned a home. After years of having worked dead-end minimum wage jobs, he was living the American dream, albeit briefly. As so often happens for middle-class blacks, Joe was among a group of laid-off workers who learned about immigration first-hand. According to reports, the day after Joe lost his job, a truckload of Mexicans were bused to the plant and hired at a considerably lower wage to do the work that Joe and scores of other American workers had been doing. Because of Joe's educational deficiencies, he was unable to get other employment at comparable wages. Financial tensions quickly caused his marriage to deteriorate, and he eventually lost his wife, their home, and his sense of dignity. Unfortunately, Joe's story is repeated all over the South, as illegal immigrants are hired and used to displace low-skill, low-wage native workers. Many of them are African-American men like Joe, legal Hispanics, and working-class whites.

Currently, there are an estimated six to seven million illegal immigrants working in low-wage, low-skill positions that could be filled by U.S.-born workers with high school educations or less. A detailed breakdown of U.S. Census unemployment data released by the Center for Immigration Studies in February 2009 reveals startling levels of unemployment for U.S.-born blacks and Hispanics without a high school education. Blacks had a 24.7 percent unemployment rate and Hispanics were at 16.2 percent. Meanwhile, the unemployment rate for legal and illegal immigrants without a high school education was 10.6 percent.

It can be argued that illegal immigration is a form of theft in which the longest law-breakers should be given the harshest penalties—not membership rights. Instead of being rewarded with amnesty, perhaps they should be fined, sent home, and placed at the end of the line. Immigration law should favor those immigrants who have shown respect for the rule of law and those who have made good-faith efforts to comply with its rules and regulations. I would place into this category those immigrants who have fallen into illegal status due to no fault of their own.

We have the technology, but not the will, to address the problem of illegal immigration. We could identify illegal workers by using the Department of Homeland Security's E-Verify system. E-Verify is a highly effective voluntary program, which allows employers to check Social Security numbers against a national database. It has a 99.6 percent accuracy rate and can yield results in a few seconds. Unfortunately, the Obama Administration has not supported the expansion of the program, which is scheduled to expire in a few months. E-Verify should be extended indefinitely and made mandatory for all employers. This would protect workers like Joe Johnson from unfair competition from an unauthorized resident such as Miguel Sanchez, who has used fake documents to claim a job that would otherwise be held by a person authorized to work in this county. Without surplus laborers, U.S. employers would be forced to raise wages in many industries and offer employees better working conditions.

Carens and other amnesty advocates should apply their considerable intellectual prowess and compassionate hearts to the plight of millions of American citizens and legal immigrants who struggle at the margins of society and who have few advocates other than some mostly Republican members of Congress and media figures such as Lou Dobbs and Fox's Glenn Beck. Indeed, I have a dream of one day living in a society where elites apply the compassion offered illegal immigrants to their fellow citizens, especially citizens who continue to suffer racial discrimination, wanton neglect, and outright rejection, even while America celebrates the election of its first black president.

Douglas S. Massey

JOSEPH CARENS HAS ADVANCED A STRONG
moral argument in favor of amnesty for irregular migrants in the United States. I agree
with the need for some kind of legalization
program and share his ethical concerns. The
current immigration crisis, however, stems
from deeper U.S. policy failures that must be
addressed, or the problem of undocumented
migration will simply recreate itself.

The core of the U.S. immigration dilemma is Mexico. Of the roughly eleven million people in the United States with undocumented status, about 60 percent—some 6.5 million people—come from Mexico. The next closest case is El Salvador, with around 570,000 undocumented migrants, followed by Guatemala at 400,000; the numbers drop off rapidly from there. If we deal effectively with migration from Mexico, other immigration problems become small by comparison and much easier to resolve.

The roots of the Mexican problem go back to 1965, when the U.S. Congress ended a 22-year-old temporary worker agreement with Mexico and enacted a new cap on immigration from the Western Hemisphere. This measure was followed in 1976 by updated country-specific limits. In a few short years, Mexico went from enjoying access to 450,000 annual guest worker visas and an unlimited number of residence visas to having no guest worker visas at all and just 20,000 visas for permanent residence.

The number of migrants entering the United States from Mexico did not change very much after 1965. What changed was their legal status. Before that year there was no significant undocumented migration to the United States, but afterward the population grew steadily to reach an estimated five million in 1986.

The Immigration Reform and Control Act (IRCA) was enacted in 1986 to deal with the emerging immigration crisis in three ways: legalizing former undocumented migrants, tightening border enforcement, and criminalizing undocumented hiring. Despite the long history of Mexico-U.S. migration and the obvious demand for Mexican workers in the United States, the law made no provision for the legal entry of additional residents or workers.

The lack of provision for legal movement was especially counterproductive because Mexico and the United States were drawing together economically. By 1994 the two countries had signed a joint agreement to lower barriers to the cross-border movement of goods, capital, information, services, commodities, and certain classes of people. But within the newly integrated North American economy, the United States refused to recognize the movement of labor. Instead in 1993 and 1994 the Border Patrol launched a series of police actions to blockade the nation's busiest border sectors.

The result was predictable. After falling to around two million in the wake of IRCA, the undocumented population quickly began to grow again thanks to the lack of legal avenues for entry. In response the United States further militarized its southern border, increasing the Border Patrol's budget by a factor of ten between 1986 and 2002 and raising the number of agents fivefold by 2008.

In the context of ongoing economic integration within North America and continued labor demand from the United States, this militarization of the border did not reduce the number of undocumented entries from Mexico. What it did do was dramatically lower the number of undocumented exits.

Militarizing the border increased the costs and risks of undocumented border crossing, and migrants quite logically adapted to this new reality by minimizing border crossing. But not by deciding to remain in Mexico. Instead, they hunkered down in the United States once they had run the gauntlet at the border.

In response to tightened border enforcement, undocumented emigration from the United States was halved. By making no provision for the movement of workers within North America and militarizing the border with our second-largest trading partner, U.S. policy did not merely fail—it backfired, actually doubling the net inflow of undocumented migrants to produce today's population of eleven million.

Although legalizing undocumented migrants may be a moral imperative, an amnesty will not by itself solve the underlying problem of undocumented migration. Mexico is a trillion-dollar economy with 110 million people, and it is a friendly nation with which we are increasingly integrated socially and economically. Yet in terms of immigration policy we treat Mexico like any other nation, allocating to it the same number of visas as to Botswana or Nepal. In the absence of legal means to accommodate the legitimate demands for work and residence visas, the flow has been diverted to unauthorized channels.

If undocumented migration is to be solved in the long term, we must address the realities of North American economic integration by providing for the legal movement of workers between Mexico and the United States. Increasing the number of permanent-residence visas and once again making temporary labor visas accessible to Mexican workers is the greater part of that effort.

This policy makes practical as well as moral sense, given that many jobs in the United States are seasonal or do not provide earnings sufficient to support American-based workers in a competitive global economy. Moreover, contrary to what most Americans think, the vast majority of Mexicans do not migrate with the intention of settling permanently in the United States. Instead they come to work temporarily in order to accumulate savings or generate remittances to solve an economic problem at home. If they had their druthers, most would return home after one or two periods of short-term U.S. labor. Militarizing the border with Mexico only frustrates the natural desire of migrants to circulate rather than settle, driving up the costs of immigration to the citizens of both countries.

Linda Bosniak

IN ANY POLICY DEBATE ON THE RIGHTS of undocumented noncitizens in liberal democratic societies, I will happily enlist Joe Carens to represent me. I agree with him that community membership must be treated as grounded in social fact rather than formal state-given status. I agree that to treat a group of residents as nonmembers undermines liberal democratic commitments, and that both principle and common sense require regularization of out-of-status immigrants. Still, I believe that his core argument—that time matters morally—raises more complications in this setting than he allows, and this is what I will explore here.

On Carens's account, unauthorized immigrants should be granted amnesty when "they have been settled for a long time." The requirement of lengthy settlement is a concession to the view held by "most people" that the political community has the right to determine its own membership. I say this is a concession because Carens became well known in the 1980s for advancing a stringent liberal critique of borders. A decade later he exchanged what he calls "idealism" for a more "realistic" approach to moral theory, one fueled by the conviction that "whatever we say ought to be done about international migration should not be too far from what we think actually might happen [and from] what we think our community might do."* This shift toward realism has entailed, here and elsewhere, his qualified acceptance of the view that states are entitled to control their membership.

As a result, for Carens, the moral claim to regularization requires more of an immigrant than just showing up. Indeed, showing up without authorization is a "wrong." Instead, the claim requires staying. And the moral character of time is such that more of it increases the power of the claim; as Carens writes, "the longer the stay, the stronger the moral claim to remain."

Undoubtedly, this emphasis on time is a crucial corrective to a formalist preoccupation with assigned legal status. Its value lies in its moral attention to context and relationship. On its premise, when a person inhabits a society

---

* Carens, Joseph H. "Realistic and Idealistic Approaches to the Ethics of Migration." *International Migration Review*, 30, no. 1 (1996): 156–170.

for some period, she develops affiliations, ties, and identifications, which change the moral calculus. Residence over the course of time produces a social membership, which at some point trumps lack of legal status, thereby both justifying and requiring regularization.

But will this time claim bear so much weight? There is, first of all, the arbitrariness involved in drawing lines as to number of years. Also troubling is the fact that time is not always an ideal proxy for affiliations and stakes. Carens acknowledges each of these concerns. But there are other difficulties, related to the fact that, as Carens himself recognizes, this time-matters argument "cuts in both directions." It embodies not only an inclusive ethic but also an exclusive one since, on his account, there is "some period of time before this [temporal] threshold is crossed" when the migrant's moral claim has not yet come to fruition, and when lack of formal status still trumps whatever de facto membership may have developed. Wherever the bar is set (whether at five years or ten), there will be some who fall short of it.

Carens's approach, in short, presupposes a class of people who are territorially present but have not been here long enough to pass into the privileged group. What of them? Assuming continued restrictive state immigration policies, and assuming also these policies' continued failures, as Carens does, this will be a constantly self-replenishing category.

Although, on his account, these shorter-term immigrants do not yet have a claim for automatic regularization, I am certain that Carens will not argue that they are beyond the protection of law in other respects. As a liberal democrat, he will insist that individuals who are present in the national territory, simply by virtue of that presence, are entitled to due process and equal protection, to marry and divorce, to own and transfer property, to make and enforce contracts, to worship freely, to send their children to school. He will insist, in short, that even those irregular migrants who fall short of the regularization threshold be recognized as legal subjects in the market and in civil society.

If so, Carens's stance is self-contradictory. These immigrants' lack of eligibility for regularization means that, all else aside, they remain subject to the state's power to deport. Carens here not only assumes but affirms this. Yet if we know anything about the lives of irregular immigrants, we know that their vulnerability to deportation functions to undercut those basic rights that are formally available to them. Indeed, the subordinating effect of deportability is the core reason (along with the need to ensure them eventual political voice) that regularization is so essential. Allowing for actual or threatened deportation of shorter-term unauthorized immigrants is, in practical terms, tantamount to nullifying many of the rights and protections that are formally extended. It is to render these immigrants, in many respects, beyond the pale. Carens fails to acknowledge that his simultaneous commitment to immigrant empowerment and the state's deportation authority will often work at cross-purposes.

There is another difficulty as well. Carens's conception of immigrants' "social membership"—a condition he treats as the normative precondition for amnesty—also falls short theoretically. Here is why: while the marginalization and subordination worked by the threat of deportation structures immigrants' lives fundamentally, the marginalization and subordination are not complete. Liberal societies treat these immigrants as civic and legal subjects in many respects—as entitled to buy and sell, gather and worship, recreate and procreate. And it is precisely by virtue of this legal recognition that immigrants are able construct the social membership that Carens emphasizes. It is this de facto membership—in neighborhoods, in schools, in families, in churches, in the marketplace and even ("even," given employer-sanction rules) in workplaces—which will eventually constitute sufficient grounds for their claim to amnesty.

There are two points to underline here. The first is that Carens's analytical severance of social membership and legal membership is misleading. What is key is that the immigrants' social membership is not prior to, or independent of, the state's law but, in many respects, a product of it. While he is right to say that "social membership does not depend upon official permission" to stay, such membership *does* depend in important respects on official recognition of these individuals' rights and standing in the market and civil society during their stay.

Arguably this makes liberal states indeed "complicit" in the process of unauthorized migration—a claim Carens disparages. They are complicit, however, not because they opportunistically encourage or tolerate irregular migration (though I think there is sometimes merit to this claim), but rather, because they make possible, via liberal legal rules, the development of immigrants' social membership in the first place.

Of course, this argument risks encouraging those who would deny all civil and social rights to undocumented aliens from the outset. After all, they will argue, it is self-defeating to guarantee rights such as property ownership and educational access that will serve to nurture ties that will later, in bootstrapping fashion, insulate the immigrants from efforts to expel them. In response, however, one can argue that allowing for a resident caste of unprotected, uneducated "pariahs" (as Owen Fiss called it in a 1998 *Boston Review* article) not only harms all of us, but also violates our deepest principles:

it is simply unacceptable, on liberal democratic grounds, to maintain a system of internal institutionalized caste.

The second point is that Carens' characterization of our shared moral convictions regarding the significance of time is incomplete. Those fundamental liberal (or, more precisely, liberal-nationalist) constitutional norms that protect the undocumented are grounded in the conviction that all persons within the state's jurisdiction are to be accorded fundamental rights, security, and recognition. For purposes of this commitment, length of stay is irrelevant; what counts is being territorially present and subject to law. Thus, whatever moral significance we might believe time ought to have for purposes of full political incorporation, the reality is that the social membership triggering the amnesty right in Carens's argument is enabled by a set of normative commitments embodied in law in which time is irrelevant.

To return to the policy question, and in conclusion, Carens's acceptance of the deportability of shorter-stay unauthorized immigrants follows from his pragmatic allowance in this essay that states maintain the right to control membership. But as a practical matter, borders often end up trumping core liberal commitments—not just at the state's frontiers, but also in the interior itself. Carens may say that this is the price of doing realistic, policy-relevant theory. There are limits to what can be publicly argued and hoped for; tradeoffs are inevitable. His concern here is to convince skeptics that long-term immigrants have any claim to regularization at all. The time argument is powerful in this setting.

But Carens's approach obscures analytically some of the complexities of undocumented immigrants' status in liberal democratic settings. And his political realism comes at the expense of forceful social criticism. Carens demands too little of the state morally. The rhetorical and political compromises entailed make me miss the early Carens—the idealistic champion of open borders.

Jean Bethke Elshtain

JOSEPH CARENS'S DEFENSE OF AMNESTY for irregular migrants is written with generosity of spirit and purpose. It helped me understand why incessant repetition of the term "illegal immigrants" is so grating, being one aspect of an increasingly pointless debate pitting often-hysterical anti-"illegals" on one side and advocates of open borders—who insist that people can come and go as they please and receive the full provision of services and panoply of rights available to legal citizens, minus citizenship obligations—on the other. Anyone troubled by the extreme rhetoric on both sides of this debate will greet his essay as a breath of fresh air.

I am one of the many Americans who remains in intimate contact with an immigrant past. My maternal grandparents of blessed memory were "Volga Germans," ethnic Germans who had made their home in Russia for centuries but were in increasing danger of having the autonomy of their communities eroded. Had they remained in Russia, they would either have been murdered under Stalin or been sent on the "long march" into the Asiatic republics of the Soviet Union, with many perishing en route. The assault on the Volga Germans was a small genocide as twentieth-century genocides go, but a genocide nonetheless. As the granddaughter of immigrants, I am keenly aware of the importance of immigration to American identity and the American experience. Should we become inhospitable to immigration, we would be an entirely different country.

That said, uncontrolled immigration poses real problems. These problems are particularly acute, as Carens points out, for liberal democracies that must refrain from certain extreme actions—for example, mass deportation of illegal or, better, irregular migrants—that would constitute a massive violation of the core principles of such democracies. Carens's proposal—accepting irregular migrants as members of the community if they have been present for an extended period—seems an attractive option. Initially, I thought that some penalty should, perhaps, be attached for having been an irregular migrant for an extended period of time. But, for the life of me, I could not think of one that would be appropriate. Dealing with the daily fears that haunt the lives of irregular migrants seemed penalty enough.

Carens's judicious approach recognizes, as the advocacy of the easy border-crossing camp does not, that a state has the "right to determine whom it will admit and to apprehend and deport migrants who settle without official authorization." At least "most people" think so, he adds as a caveat. I would cast this right in stronger language for it is a recognized feature of what it means to be a sovereign state. Carens is correct that that right, like any right, is not and can never be absolute. What he proposes is to soften that right and to explore whether the state incurs moral obligations to irregular migrants over a period of time. He makes a powerful case on behalf of this view.

To be sure, the stories of those he chooses to illustrate his position were no doubt selected because they are particularly poignant and powerful. Any but the hardest of the hard-hearted will understand the rationale for regularizing the presence of such persons among us. But suppose someone has slithered along for the requisite time Carens suggests—five to seven years—selling illegal drugs, participating in gang activities, trafficking in stolen goods. Do we incur a moral obligation to this sort of irregular migrant? Surely not. The irregular migrants he describes are those who can make a reasonable claim that the United States has become their home; that they are law-abiding members of the society; and that, therefore, their de facto presence should generate a de jure right to remain. The sheer number of years is not by itself decisive.

Carens's essay is not the work of one interested in rewarding lawbreaking. Were that the case, he would surely go for blanket amnesties to be issued every few years. Instead, he calls for a certain form of recognition of what a person does over a span of time during which he or she works, pays taxes, goes to school, perhaps starts a family, and does not run afoul of the law except insofar as he or she is present without authorization. It has never made sense to me to treat all such persons as criminals, a point Carens makes. Given our messy, conflicted immigration situation at present, his moderation is welcome. I do, however, see some difficulties. Let me mention two; one is pragmatic, the other conceptual.

First, it would require considerable finesse and care on the part of officials to weigh the cases and avoid regularizing the presence of those who have by no means made America their home so much as the place they have exploited for shady purposes. Careful procedures would need to be drawn up. By retraining those who are currently devoted to ferreting out "illegals," we could avoid adding another layer of inefficient bureaucracy to our existing immigration control efforts. I may be overstating the difficulties, given that the irregular migrants Carens has in mind do not have to prove anything other than their presence among us for a given period of time as law-abiding persons who are working and raising families. But if his criterion is not just the passage of time, as he insists, but what was done over that span of time, officials must be provided the means to make important distinctions.

Since what was done matters, we face a conceptual problem. It cannot be enough simply to acknowledge that some irregular migrants have successfully taken advantage of the U.S. job market while avoiding the law. This is too calculating and utilitarian an approach. Carens should tie amnesty to aspirations for freedom and legal equality, as it was for my grandparents and so many others over the years. Those dimensions cannot be ignored: they are central to the American ideal of what it means to be a free citizen of a republic.

In light of this second concern, I propose an addition to Carens's argument. Those whose status is changed from "irregular" to "legal" will be obliged to take the citizenship classes now incumbent upon legal immigrants who become citizens. The waiting period for legal residents is five years. The waiting period for irregular migrants should also be at least five years. A ritual of citizenship and recognition of membership are vital—hence the obligation to study, to pass the test, and to take one's oath as a full-fledged citizen. Anyone who has made the United States his or her home should not cavil at such a requirement. I recall tutoring my grandmother in civics when she decided, in her 60s, to become a citizen at long last. The citizen granddaughter tutoring the non-citizen grandmother whose life had made the granddaughter's possible was, for me, a touching experience, and it reminded me of how much I owed to my unlettered and impoverished grandparents. As children, they came to this bewilderingly complex country and made it their home—in every sense of the word. We should never underestimate or ignore the power of this process.

T. Alexander Aleinikoff

JOSEPH CARENS DESCRIBES SEVERAL IN-
dividual cases that are poignant and worthy of remedy. But exactly why the United
States—its Congress or people—have a
moral obligation to assist undocumented
migrants is under-argued. Carens refers to
a number of possible lines of analysis but
never settles on a particular argument; he
is letting the obvious inhumanity of the

treatment of Miguel Sanchez, Margaret Grimmond, and Hiu Lui Ng do the work for him. It is "morally wrong," we are told,

> to force someone to leave the place where she was raised, where she received her social formation, and where she has her most important human connections, just because her parents brought her there without official authorization.

What justifies this intuition?

Carens offers several arguments. First, he makes a *claim from membership*. That can be worked out in two ways. The first focuses on social facts: long-term undocumented migrants have made the United States their home; indeed, for those who arrived as children (the so-called 1.5 generation), they really may know no other home. They belong, in two senses of the word: they belong in the United States and they belong to American society. Deportation strips long-term residents of this membership, separating them from family and community. If these are the kinds of ties that make life meaningful and pleasurable, that help us flourish as human beings, then there is a moral argument against policies that undermine them.

The claim from membership also has an equal-protection dimension. If long-term undocumented residents are, in effect, members, and if we do not deport citizens, then to remove some members but not other, similarly situated members would be arbitrary. This kind of argument held sway in the 1982 case *Plyler v. Doe*, in which the Supreme Court found unconstitutional a Texas statute barring undocumented children from public schools. According to the majority opinion, these children would in all likelihood become members of our society; to deny them education would create, in effect, a caste of second-class members.

A second argument Carens employs is a *claim from family.* As Carens notes, family life is deemed a fundamental human right. Article 16 of the Universal Declaration of Human Rights states: "The family is the natural and fundamental group unit of society and is entitled to protection by society and the State." To deport a long-term undocumented resident is likely to severely undermine the exercise of that right in the United States. This argument has received some play under European human rights instruments, but it has not carried weight in the United States. Adjudicators have worried about the incentives it creates for undocumented migration. Furthermore, deportation does not destroy family unity; it may simply require it to take place in another country.

Carens's third line of argument is a *claim from proportionality.* He writes that to "uproot a person who has spent fifteen or twenty years as a contributing member of society" would be "cruel and inhumane": "The harm is entirely out of proportion to the wrong of illegal entry." This appears to be an extension, or restatement, of the claim from membership. In any event, how one quantifies the "wrong of illegal entry" is not further elaborated upon, nor is the concept of proportionality linked to a deeper moral theory.

I am not sure which of these arguments Carens thinks carries the day—or perhaps his view is that all of them add up to a strong moral claim. They may well. But without full development of the underlying moral theories it is difficult to know.

Making the case for relief from removal on somewhat more prosaic policy grounds may be more fruitful. It is common for countries' immigration laws to provide avenues—written into statute or established through the exercise of administrative discretion—for unauthorized migrants to remain when the harm to them, their family, and the community significantly outweighs the harm of illegal entry and where there are no other strong grounds warranting removal (such as the commission of a serious criminal offense). As Carens notes, U.S. law has for some time included a statute that permits case-by-case determinations of this kind; the law was unduly tightened in 1996, when Congress added the requirement that undocumented migrants seeking relief from removal demonstrate that their removal would result in "exceptional and extremely unusual hardship" to a close family member who is a U.S. citizen or green-card holder.

Carens seeks more than discretionary intervention, arguing for a rolling statute of limitations available to undocumented migrants who have spent a significant length of time in the United States. Such a rule is likely to be over-inclusive and under-inclusive, but this lack of fit may be justified on administrative grounds—again as a matter of policy. An even broader form of relief is possible, and it has received the greatest attention in recent immigration debates: legalization for undocumented migrants, even those who have been here a relatively short period of time, provided they pay a fine, learn English, have paid their taxes, and have not committed a serious crime.

For all these proposals, moral claims can be made on both sides. The social facts of undocumented life may be said to create a kind of membership that has moral weight, but there is also the moral claim of a self-governing people to determine who should be members of their polity—a claim that might not diminish in significance simply because an unlawful entrant has evaded detection for some length of time (the dissenting justices in *Plyler* made precisely this point: the presence of the undocumented children in Texas schools had never been consented to by "We the People" or our elected officials). Or the moral claim from proportionality that argues for relief from removal can be compared to the moral claim of those who wait patiently in line outside the United States—some for many years; people who, had they entered illegally, could have established the kind of ties in the United States that are now said to justify legal status for the queue jumpers. Indeed, I worry that the attempt to make the argument on moral grounds could jeopardize the chance for a solution that would aid the persons Carens cares about, as opponents line up moral claims on the other side.

Pragmatic arguments may, in the end, be the most persuasive. For the long-term undocumented residents about whom Carens writes, Congress ought to return the law to its pre-1996 form. Congress should also adopt a general legalization program: the U.S. government simply is not going to send home eleven million undocumented residents—the costs of enforcement would be too high, the clamor from communities would be too great—whether or not the American people recognize a powerful moral claim that they be permitted to remain. Legalization has its costs in terms of providing incentives to enter illegally and expanding eligibility for social programs. But on balance these costs are likely to be outweighed by the benefits of protecting against exploitation and promoting integration into American society.

ABOUT THE CONTRIBUTORS

Joseph H. Carens is Professor of Political Science at the University of Toronto and author of four previous books, including *Culture, Citizenship, and Community*. He is completing a book on the ethics of immigration, *Who Belongs? Immigration, Democracy, and Citizenship*.

T. Alexander Aleinikoff, United Nations Deputy High Commissioner for Refugees and Professor of Law at Georgetown University, is author of *Semblances of Sovereignty: The Constitution, the State, and American Citizenship*.

Linda Bosniak is Professor of Law at Rutgers University Law School and author of *The Citizen and the Alien: Dilemmas of Contemporary Membership*.

JEAN BETHKE ELSHTAIN, Laura Spelman Rockefeller Professor of Social and Political Ethics at the University of Chicago, is author of many books, including *Public Man, Private Woman* and *God, the State, and Self*.

DOUGLAS S. MASSEY is Henry G. Bryant Professor of Sociology and Public Affairs at Princeton University and coauthor of *American Apartheid* and *Miracles on the Border*.

MAE M. NGAI, Professor of History and Lung Family Professor of Asian American Studies at Columbia University, is author of *Impossible Subjects: Illegal Aliens and the Making of Modern America*.

CAROL M. SWAIN is Professor of Political Science and Law at Vanderbilt University and editor of *Debating Immigration*. Her Web site is carolmswain.com.

BOSTON REVIEW BOOKS

Boston Review Books is an imprint of *Boston Review*, a bimonthly magazine of ideas. The book series, like the magazine, is animated by hope, committed to equality, and convinced that the imagination eludes political categories. Visit bostonreview.net for more information.